TORNADO ALLEY

by
Tami
Brumbaugh

BEACON HILL PRESS
OF KANSAS CITY

Copyright © 2015
by Beacon Hill Press of Kansas City

Printed in the United States of America

ISBN: 978-0-8341-3473-7

Cover Design: Doug Bennett
Illustrator: Doug Bennett
Interior Design: Sharon Page
Editor: William Rolfe

Author's Note: This is based on a true story. Justin and his family are excited about summer vacation approaching. He is rehearsing for the sixth-grade graduation at Plaza Towers Elementary when sirens begin to blast. The teachers lead their students to the safest places available in the school. Justin prays for God's protection, but the tornado still demolishes Plaza Towers and much of Moore, Oklahoma. This Advanced-reader children's book is part of the *Passport to Missions* curriculum for 2015-16.

10 9 8 7 6 5 4 3 2 1

Dedication

To Moore, Oklahoma residents who battled a tornado,
and to compassionate people throughout the
United States who decided to help.

Contents

1. Hide and Seek   5

2. It's Here   10

3. Flipped Car   16

4. Cartoon Arm   22

5. Bandages   28

6. Missing   34

7. Action Hero   39

8. Prayer Request   44

9. Lost and Found   49

Discussion Questions   56

1
Hide and Seek

Juniper bush branches quivered, drawing attention to three sets of eyes gleaming in the shadows. Justin froze in his tracks and stifled his breathing. Faint thumping sounds began and more branches shook.

Justin spun around and dashed behind the house. No one followed. He crept through his back yard, careful not to step on any twigs or gravel. A robin burst out of the grass in front of him, grasping a worm firmly in her beak. He paused, looking over his shoulder. Could he make it without being noticed?

He peeked around the corner and studied the back view of the juniper bushes. Two sets of bare, scratched legs poked out of the branches. A few feet away, a curled tail whipped back and forth, thumping in excitement.

"He didn't see us this time," whispered one voice.

"That's 'cuz we're such good hiders," another voice whispered back.

Justin grinned and tiptoed closer. The tail stopped wagging and disappeared, replaced by a black, flat nose and shining eyes. Justin grabbed his brother and sister's legs and pulled them out of the bushes. They

5

screamed until they saw Justin, and then began gig-gling.

Their tan pug jumped up and down on his stubby legs, yapping and snorting. Justin scratched the dog's wrinkled head. "You like this game, don't you, Tank?"

Tank wagged his curled tail, shaking his entire compact, square body. He licked Justin's hand.

"All of you are too easy to find," Justin said. "You need to find new hiding places."

"But there aren't any new hiding places," said Sophie. She pushed her black curls out of her face.

"Yeah, we've hidden everywhere. You need to get badder at finding us," four-year-old Brady stated. He wiped a clump of mud off his new red super hero shirt.

"Maybe the three of you should split up. Some-times Tank's tail gives you away."

"But that's not as much fun," Sophie said. "Besides, Tank doesn't like being alone. He would just follow us."

Mom opened the back door. "Do you guys have your homework done?"

Justin and Sophie groaned.

"I didn't think so. I told you to finish it Saturday, so you could relax today." Mom opened the door wider. "Everybody inside."

Tank snorted and scampered into the house. The kids followed slowly.

Brady smiled. "I don't have homework."

"Once you're in third grade you will," said Sophie. "I get lots of it."

"Not as much as me. Sixth graders get it all the time. Of course, that's why I'm so much smarter than you two." Justin grinned.

"I'm smart, too," Brady said. "I can sing my ABC song faster than anybody else in my preschool. Watch me."

He hopped on one foot, and then the other, chanting his ABC song. He only forgot the "m" and the "t". Mom clapped, and they sang the song together, with all of the letters.

Brady stuck out his chest. "See? Smart."

Mom smiled and patted his back. Her smile faded. "Is that mud on your new shirt? Didn't I tell you to change out of your good clothes right when we got home from church?"

Brady hung his head. "I just forgot."

"I think you manage to stain something at least once a week. Let's see if we can actually go a few days keeping our clothes clean. Go change," Mom commanded. "And the rest of you, get to work."

Justin trudged up the stairs. "I don't think I can study anymore. We should be done with tests by now."

"Come on," said Mom. "Finish strong. Just a few more days."

"Five more days," Sophie corrected. "That's thirty-five more hours. I've been keeping track."

"I don't want school to be over," said Brady. "We do fun stuff."

"Maybe YOU don't want it to be over but I'm ready for a break," Justin said. "Besides, the quicker we get done with school, the quicker we get to go to Florida. I can't wait!"

"Florida! Florida!" Sophie chanted.

"Can I wear floaties at the beach?" asked Brady.

"Yes," said Mom.

"Can I wear my shark swimming suit?" Brady questioned.

"Yes," Mom answered.

"Can I wear my green goggles?"

"Yes."

"Can I play with some sharks?"

"No."

"How about an octopus?"

"No."

Justin escaped to his room and shut the door. His brother's question-asking sessions could last a *long* time. He pulled out his math assignment and flopped onto his bed. After struggling through two problems, he found himself staring out the window. Gray clouds were crowding out the blue sky. He shrugged. At least if it rained, he wouldn't wish he was outside on his bike instead of stuck doing homework. Ugh! He returned to his math.

* * *

The next morning, Justin awoke with a start. He looked at his alarm clock and groaned. How many times had he hit the snooze button? He showered quickly and threw on khaki shorts and a black T-shirt. He finger-combed his hair as he stomped down the stairs for breakfast. His mom was already serving scrambled eggs and toast.

Brady squirted ketchup onto his eggs in a smiley-face design. He glanced down at his new Captain America shirt to make sure it did not have ketchup on it. "You'd better hurry," he said with his mouth full.

"Yeah," added Sophie. She adjusted a purple polka-dotted headband in her hair. "We're almost done eating."

Justin sat at the kitchen table and began stuffing eggs into his mouth. No time to smear jelly on his toast. He folded the bread and jammed it into his mouth.

"You're going to choke," Sophie commented.

Dad carried his dishes to the sink. "I'm off to work. Be good at school."

"Bye, Daddy," said Brady. "Be good at work."

Mom and Sophie hugged Dad. Tank jumped at his feet, wagging his curled tail. Justin just waved. His mouth was still full of toast and eggs. If only he had known it would be the last meal his family would eat together in their home.

2
It's Here

A stifled sob caused Justin to raise his eyebrows in surprise. Lauren sat beside him wiping her eyes and sniffing.

"Why are you crying?" he whispered.

"I'm not crying," Lauren snapped. Students on either side of them turned to stare. She softened her voice. "OK, so I'm crying a little. You don't need to tell the world."

"I wasn't trying to. I'm the one who whispered, remember?" Justin said, turning back to face the front.

She sighed. "I guess that's true." She sniffed again. "It's just . . . strange to be sitting here. I mean, I'm glad to graduate. I'm just . . . sad to leave Plaza Towers. I've gone to school here since kindergarten."

"Yeah, me too."

"I'm looking forward to going to Highland West Junior High. I mean, we're practically seventh graders. It's time to move on."

Justin nodded. Why was she still talking?

"It'll be fun going to a different school. We'll have lots of teachers, and lockers and . . . What if I can't remember my locker combination? Maybe I don't want to leave elementary school."

10

"Everyone stand up, please," instructed Ms. Jones.

Justin breathed a sigh of relief. Music began to play and the sixth-grade students started to walk toward their graduation spots. He felt a surge of pride as he strolled past the "Home of the Panthers" banner. Lauren glanced at the sign and choked back more sobs. Justin shook his head.

Thunder crashed and the lights flickered. A few kids jumped, but the music continued playing so the students kept walking. Hail started to pelt the skylights. Some kids stopped to listen. Suddenly, a siren blared in the distance. Startled, everyone looked to their teachers for instructions. Was it another drill? It seemed strange to do a drill during graduation practice. The music stopped. An eerie hush fell over the room.

The voice of Principal Simpson rang out over the intercom. "Teachers, please get your students to their protected areas. This is not a drill."

Justin's heart began to pound. The kids around him started to chatter in panicked voices.

"Not a drill?" Lauren said. "Is this real? Is a tornado coming?"

"Voices off," Ms. Bromley commanded. "Follow your teacher to the boy's bathroom."

"Stay calm," added Ms. Brim. "We'll be fine. Just stay in line."

The three sixth-grade teachers herded their classes down the hall and through the bathroom door. Their footsteps echoed down the hall.

"How are all of us supposed to fit in here?" asked one student.

"We'll make it work," said Ms. Jones. "I know it's tight, but we need to get into position."

"Eww," Lauren exclaimed. "On the bathroom floor? Couldn't we go to the girl's bathroom? It's much cleaner."

"Fifth-grade needs that bathroom. Quickly now," said Ms. Brim.

Justin's legs felt like rubber. He was glad to drop to his knees. All of the students crouched into the defensive position they had practiced repeatedly since kindergarten. They bent toward their knees and automatically clasped hands over their heads for protection.

While on his knees, it felt only natural for Justin to pray. He squeezed his eyes shut. "Please God, keep us safe and make the tornado leave us alone."

"I'm glad you're praying," said Lauren. "I've never prayed before, but my parents told me about a tornado that hit Moore right before we were born. It tore everything up and killed lots of people. We could all die."

"Thanks for the encouragement," Justin said. He felt a knot form in his stomach.

The hail began to beat on the roof even harder. It sounded like they were in a tin can and someone was throwing rocks at them. The siren continued to blare.

Principal Simpson peeked in the door. "Are all of you in position?"

The sixth-grade teachers answered yes.

"I'm going to check on the other grades," she said.

Justin pictured Sophie and Brady in his mind. Were they in a safe place? Were they scared? What about his parents? He wished his entire family was together.

Lauren started crying beside him. Ms. Jones crouched down beside her and began to rub her back. "Don't worry. The tornado might not even come this way. We just need to play it safe. Are you hanging in there, Justin?"

Justin nodded.

"Hey, listen," his teacher said. She paused for a moment. "The little kids must be down the hall. I can hear them singing."

Justin cupped his ears with his hands. Faint voices were singing "Twinkle, Twinkle Little Star." Some of the kids stumbled over the words, while others sang way off key. It was a good distraction and helped his heartbeat slow down. The kids began to sing their ABC song. One voice belted out the letters much louder than the others and missed the "m" and "t." Justin grinned. He knew that voice. Brady was being brave. Justin listened closely, grateful to hear voices battle the siren and the wind. He wondered if Sophie's class stayed in the smaller building. He'd feel better if he could hear her voice too.

The intercom clicked on. Principal Simpson's panicked voice shouted, "It's here!"

Justin tensed. The pounding of hail was overshadowed by rushing wind. The siren and the singing were drowned out by what sounded like a freight train bearing down on them. Were kids screaming? Was he screaming? It was too loud to tell.

Chunks of ceiling dropped on his head. The chunks became bigger and sharper and blew down harder and harder. Ms. Jones draped herself over him and his classmates, deflecting some of the blows. Justin tried to open his eyes. The air was dark and filled with debris. A backpack flew by, followed closely by a chair. The sound of metal scraping and bending screeched above the wind. Justin wanted to plug his ears, but was afraid to take his hands off his head. He felt a huge gust of wind burst through. Where was the roof?

The mirror shattered into tiny pieces. Kids cried out as pieces of glass flew through the air, cutting their skin. Justin groaned from a searing pain on the back of his leg. Metal bathroom stalls shook violently. He peeked long enough to see a stall door ripped off its hinges and spun up into the air. He braced his head, ready for the door to slam on top of them. Instead it flew upward and disappeared in the wind and debris. He felt like a giant vacuum cleaner was sucking him upward. Ms. Jones held his arm. Lauren grabbed his elbow. His classmates huddled tightly together. They were starting to turn and lift off the ground. There was nothing else to hold on to. His eyes stung, so he clenched them shut.

"Oh, please, God. Please, God. Please, please, please. Help us, God," he repeated.

3
Flipped Car

Justin opened his eyes. The roaring beast was thundering away from them, looking for something else to devour. A horrifying hush draped over what used to be the school. He gawked at the sprawling mound of twisted metal and concrete surrounding him. Cinder block walls were punched over. The entire roof was gone. The glass front of the building was totally smashed.

"Is anyone hurt?" asked Ms. Jones.

Justin blinked in shock. Her hair was wild, her sleeves were torn and she was splattered with mud. He looked down to find that he did not look any better. He inspected his hands and legs for injury. His arms were flecked with blood. Was it his blood? He was too numb to tell. The back of his calf had a long cut. He absent-mindedly pulled up his sock to slow down the blood flow. His entire body ached and his skin felt like it had been rubbed with sand paper, but everything seemed to work. Had he actually survived a tornado in one piece?

Lauren hobbled over to Ms. Jones and hugged her. "I was so scared. I thought we were all going to die."

Ms. Jones squeezed her back. "I'm so glad you're OK. Let's look for everyone else."

They sorted through the rubble, pulling out more classmates. His friends emerged shell-shocked and shaky. Some had bulging bumps on their heads. Others had cuts and scrapes. As he looked around, he was surprised that no one standing by him was seriously hurt.

Teachers began gathering their students like mother hens, counting to see if anyone was missing. As cramped as the bathroom had been, it looked like one of the safer parts of the building. Where were his brother and sister? His brother was singing close to him during the storm. The hallway where he had found shelter should be nearby.

He climbed over a splintered desk and overturned chair. Everywhere he turned, teachers and students were pushing pieces of walls aside and pulling out shaking kids. Were his brother and sister still buried? Could they breathe?

Justin walked in the direction the singing came from before the tornado hit. A few partial walls still remained. One toppled as he passed. He jumped out of the way, inhaling dust. He coughed and sputtered, but continued searching.

"Brady!" he called.

He stopped suddenly and gasped. A car was flipped over on more collapsed walls and rubble. Could he actually be in the parking lot? He looked around. It was the only car in sight. The random power of the storm was overwhelming. He stepped closer and heard yelling.

Teachers and staff rushed to the car and peered underneath.

"Linda and Kaye are under there!" someone yelled. "I can see some kids, too."

Students jumped in to try to move the car.

"Careful! We don't want everything to collapse," said a janitor.

Justin inched closer. Was Brady's teacher named Linda? He always called her Ms. Patterson. Justin peered into the pile of debris beneath the car. Ms. Patterson looked up. Her arms were wrapped around several tiny kids. How had they managed to survive with a car on top of them?

She squeezed the kids tighter. "See? There's help. We're all going to be just fine."

"The wall is holding the car off of them," another teacher said. "If we're careful, we should be able to pull them out."

Staff members formed an assembly line. One teacher bent in and pulled a frightened preschool girl out. She was shaking as he passed her down the line. A teacher passed her to Justin. The little girl clung to him, terrified.

"You're OK now," Justin said. He patted her back awkwardly and placed her gently on a cinder block.

Another student was passed down the line and then another. Still there was no Brady.

"Did any of you see Brady down there?" he asked the preschoolers.

"I don't know," said a little girl with braids. "It was too dark in there to see."

Neighbors from nearby houses began to climb into the rubble to help find children. Sirens blared and lights flashed as ambulances and fire trucks pulled up to the school. People were shouting. Kids kept crying. Justin felt overwhelmed and confused.

"Why did You let the tornado hit us, God?" he muttered. "Doesn't the wind obey You? Why did it still hit our school? Where is my family?"

He watched the preschool kids. They huddled together trying to keep warm. A light rain dripped on them, leaving streaks on their muddy faces. Justin shook his head. Where was God in all of this?

He sighed as another kid was passed down the line. The little boy was covered in mud and wore a ripped Captain America shirt. Justin's heart pumped hard as the small body was passed closer to him.

"Brady?" he asked.

The dirty face grinned. "Hi, Justin."

His brother was finally handed to him. He squeezed him tight. Brady squeezed back.

"Did you know we were almost sucked up into a tornado?" he asked.

Justin smiled. "I figured that out. So, Captain America, were you the one holding up that car, so your class didn't get squished?"

"Even I'm not that strong," Brady answered. "That was God. He had angels all around to protect us. They made sure the car didn't crush us." He looked down at his shirt. "Oh, no!'

"What?"

"Mom told me to keep my clothes clean for once. My shirt's dirty and ripped. Think I'll be in trouble?"

Justin hugged him. "I think Mom will understand."

"So where is Sophie?" Brady asked.

Justin swallowed hard. "I haven't been able to find her yet. Let's look together."

"Where is the third-grade building?"

"I wish I knew."

The two boys pulled up battered classroom doors and peeked under mounds of rubble. A shredded purple polka-dotted headband peeked out of a pile of crushed cinder blocks.

"Sophie!" Brady shouted.

No answer.

A group of neighbors and firefighters were bunched together. Two teachers stood nearby, crying.

"I need everyone quiet for a few minutes," said one fireman. "We need to be able to hear if anyone else is alive under there."

"Is this the third-grade building?" Justin asked.

The teachers held fingers to their lips, but nodded.

"My sister is in there. I need to help."

One of the teachers blocked him. "No. Don't go over there. Some of the kids didn't . . ." She stopped, took a deep breath and then continued, ". . . you just shouldn't go over there yet."

The other teacher patted Brady's back. "Let's get you two back to your teachers. We'll let you know when they get more kids out." She walked them back to Ms. Jones and Ms. Patterson.

Ms. Jones exhaled deeply. "Justin. Oh good. I wasn't sure where you went. They want all of the older grades to go to a nearby church while we wait. It's just too crazy having so many kids here."

Justin held on to Brady. "I can't leave my brother. And we're still looking for my sister."

"Don't worry. They will join us right away. We'll just be around the corner."

"Justin! Don't go!" Brady pleaded.

"You"ll be fine," said Ms. Jones. "The preschool classes are over there." She pointed to her left. "Your teacher will want to know you're safe. You boys can meet up in a few minutes."

Brady reluctantly returned to his teacher. Justin waved helplessly as he and his classmates were herded away.

4
Cartoon Arm

The fourth, fifth, and sixth-grade students from Plaza Towers sat on the floor facing the front door of the church. The teachers tried to keep them calm, but shock was wearing off and panic was setting in. The dim lighting from the windows added to the depressing atmosphere.

Justin wrapped his arms around his legs and rocked back and forth. He pictured the demolished third grade building and the devastated expressions of everyone digging there. Was Sophie still buried? Was she hurt?

Brady was the only family member he knew had survived. How much of Moore, Oklahoma had the tornado destroyed? Had it hurt his mom and dad? What if he and Brady were the only people left in their family?

Justin covered his face with his hands and prayed. "Dear God, we need You. I don't understand why this is happening."

Lauren sat at the edge of a group of kids. She was chewing her nails. Some kids were sobbing, while others seemed dazed.

Four adults burst through the front doors, calling their children's names. The kids raced forward, leaping into their parent's outstretched arms. After hugs and inspection of wounds, the adults escorted their sons and daughters out of the church. A steady stream of parents began pouring in several minutes later.

Justin smiled for each of his friends, while keeping an eye on the door for anyone from his family. Time dragged on. He studied the clock. It was 4:00. He would normally be home from school by now. Homework seemed so tedious last night, but he would be happy to be sitting at his desk working right now. He'd even be glad to do his chores like cleaning his room or taking out the trash.

At least half of the students had now left with their parents. Justin stood up and stretched his aching muscles. The cut on his leg began to throb, but at least it was no longer bleeding. His sock slipped down but dried mud served as a Band-Aid. He slumped on the floor, glancing back and forth between the front door and the clock. Ten more minutes passed. It felt more like ten hours.

"Justin! Justin!" Brady called.

Justin jumped to his feet. Brady and Dad weaved their way around the remaining students, searching frantically. Justin ran to meet them. Dad grabbed him in a bear hug. Brady squeezed his way into the hug too.

"Are you OK?" asked Dad. "Do we need to take you to a doctor?"

"Nah. I'm just cut up a little. How are you?"

"The tornado didn't hit my office, so I wasn't hurt at all. I drove here as quickly as I could. Police stopped me about a mile from the school, so it took a while for

me to find Brady and figure out where you were." Dad hugged Justin again. "I'm so glad you aren't hurt."

"What about Mom and Sophie? Did you find them?" Justin asked.

Dad's smile faded. "I found them. Your mom drove to the school right before the tornado hit. She was going to take you guys home, but the school was already locked down. She didn't have time to get back to the house, so she ran to a neighbor's storm shelter. They let her in just in time. She's fine. Sophie . . . well, Sophie was really beat up. Mom found her in the triage center on the basketball court. The third-grade building was hit hard. You saw it, right?"

Justin and Brady nodded.

"The kids and teachers in that building . . ." Dad choked up. "Some of them are only banged up, but most are in the hospital and some of them . . ." He took a deep breath. "I'm sure Sophie will pull through. I drove her and Mom to the hospital. Moore Medical Center was destroyed, so we had to go to Norman Regional Hospital. We can go back there to see how Sophie's doing. I wanted to get here as fast as I could to make sure you were OK and weren't worrying about us."

"Thanks, Dad."

"Let's go," said Brady. "Sophie may need me to sing to her so she will wake up. It works at home, except I get in trouble for it then."

They all climbed into Dad's car.

Brady grabbed Justin's hand. "Sophie looked scary," he whispered. "She wouldn't open her eyes and her arm looked like a cartoon arm."

"A cartoon arm?"

"Yeah, zig-zaggy. Dad didn't want to scare you, but I thought you might want to know before you see her."

"Thanks. I wish you didn't have to see her looking scary."

"It's OK." Brady pointed to his muddy Captain America shirt. "I'm tough, remember? Just like a super hero."

The boys looked out their windows, shaken by the extent of the destruction. It looked like a giant lawn mower had shredded their town. Many of the buildings were stripped of all but their cement foundations. Street signs were twisted and down, and there were cars flipped on their sides or upside down. Big trees were now just stumps.

Brady closed his eyes and sank down in his seat. "I think I've seen enough scary stuff for today. My toughness is running out."

"I know what you mean."

They were silent for the rest of the drive to the hospital. Justin was anxious to see Mom and Sophie again. He hoped they had already fixed his sister's "zig-zaggy" arm. No one in his family had dealt with a broken bone before.

"We're here," Dad said.

He opened the car door for his sons, and they slid out. Injured people were limping in, some supported by friends or family, others walked on their own. Most of the people were covered in mud and storm scars. An ambulance blared its siren and flashed its lights as it pulled up in front of the main entrance. Two medics jumped out of the vehicle, still working on a patient strapped to a stretcher. Brady hid behind his dad.

"Are you two up to taking the stairs?" asked Dad. "The elevators are packed."

The boys nodded. Justin was in pain each time he took a step. The cut on his leg hurt badly, but he remained quiet. He just wanted to get to his sister's hospital room.

They rounded the corner and saw Mom sitting on a bench. Her head was between her hands as she stared at the floor.

"Mom!" Brady yelled.

She looked up and a smile spread across her muddy and tear stained face. What was left of her mascara ran down her cheeks as she stood and held out her arms. Justin and Brady ran to her.

"There you are!" she exclaimed, hugging them tight. "Oh, Justin! Brady said you were OK, but I was still so worried. Look at you! You have cuts all over. I need to have the doctor look you over."

"I'm OK, Mom. Really!"

Dad gave Mom a hug too. "How's Sophie doing?"

Mom looked up at him with tears in her eyes. "The nurse said she should be back from surgery any minute now. I'm glad you got here before she came out. There's something you should know."

5
Bandages

"What do we need to know?" asked Justin. "Is there something wrong with Sophie that the doctors can't fix?"

Dad sank into the chair. "She was unconscious and had a bump on her head. Does she have brain damage?"

"Did she break her pinky toe?" Brady asked.

"No. No, none of that," Mom said. "Her arm was broken in two places, so she'll have a cast. Her head was hit hard, so they will treat her for a concussion, but they expect her to have a full recovery. *Physically* I think the worst is over."

"Oh, Praise the Lord!" Dad exclaimed.

"So, what's the problem?" Justin asked.

"Mentally she is going to have a lot to deal with," Mom said.

"Well, yes, all of them may have nightmares and some psychological issues to get over," said Dad.

"No. It's more than that. Some of her classmates are here for surgeries too, so I've been talking with quite a few parents from Plaza Towers." Mom sighed and rubbed her head. "Her teacher, Miss Doan may be here for quite a while. She was really hurt badly. And some of the kids . . . well, some of the kids from school didn't survive. Most of them were from Sophie's class. Some of them were her close friends."

"Oh, no," said Dad.

"She doesn't know anyone died yet. The doctors thought it would be best to wait a few days before we tell her. She needs to heal a little first. I just wanted you to know before you accidentally said something about her friends in front of her."

Big tears ran down Brady's cheeks. "Some kids from our school died?"

Mom wrapped her arms around him. "Oh, honey. I'm so sorry. I shouldn't have told you either. People are talking about it so you would have heard it soon enough, but I know this has been a hard day. You are so brave."

Dad drew Justin close. "You've both been brave."

Two nurses wheeled a hospital bed toward them. A pale face with wild black curls poked out of the sheets. Dad opened the door as they wheeled the bed into the room.

"You must be Sophie's family," said a nurse with spiky blonde hair. I'm Susan and this is Tanya."

Dad nodded. "Thanks for taking care of Sophie. How is she?"

"She may be groggy for a while," Tanya said, "The anesthesia [a-ne-THE-shuh] is just now wearing off. The doctor said the surgery went very well. She'll be in a cast for quite a while and we're going to keep her hooked up to IVs for the night and monitor her concussion. Other than that, she's looking good."

"Thank you," said Mom.

"No problem," Susan said.

The nurses hooked up Sophie's IV and checked her chart. They tucked the white sheet around her and adjusted her pillow.

"If you need anything else . . . Hold on a minute," said Susan. She stepped closer to Justin and Brady. "You look like you were in the tornado too. Has anyone checked you out yet?"

Each boy shook his head.

"It looks like we may need some bandages. Can you boys go wash up a little in the bathroom while we get some supplies?" Susan asked. "We'll be right back."

Mom poured warm water on a washcloth and began gently scrubbing Brady's arms. Justin splashed water on his face and rubbed it with soap. It stung in his cuts. By the time their arms, legs and faces were clean, several white washcloths and towels were *extremely* dirty.

The nurses returned and set a tray full of supplies on the night stand.

"OK, little man," said Tanya. "You are first. Do you have a name, or do you go strictly by Captain America?"

Brady smiled. "You can just call me Captain."

"His name is Brady," said Dad.

"But I like the name Captain."

"Captain it is. Does anything hurt?" asked Nurse Tanya.

"I'm kinda sore all over, but I'm not really bleeding. My teacher stood over us. She and God and the angels worked together and held a car off of me and my friends."

"Is that so?" the nurse laughed. "Is she Wonder Woman?"

"Actually," said Justin, "that part is true. I saw them under the flipped car."

Nurse Tanya's eyes widened. "Wow, then I would say you have a lot to be thankful for."

"Yep," said Brady.

"I'm just going to clean some scratches, but otherwise you look surprisingly well, Captain."

"Your turn young man," said Susan. "And you are . . ."

"Justin."

"Well, Justin. You may have gotten a little more damage, but nothing a few bandages can't fix. Wait. Hold on—except for this cut on your leg. I think we may need a few stitches for that one."

"Is he going to look like Frankenstein?" asked Brady.

"Sorry to disappoint you, but I think this will just be a small scar."

Susan rubbed an orange antiseptic on the wound and gave Justin a numbing shot. Mom escorted Brady out of the room, informing him that they needed to get some food. Dad offered Justin a hand to squeeze and had him look at his face. Within a few minutes, his leg was stitched and bandaged.

"Much better," said Susan.

The nurses cleaned up their supplies and checked on Sophie again.

"All her vitals are good," said Tanya. "If you need anything else, just press the red call button."

"Thanks," said Dad.

"Yeah, thanks," Justin said. His leg felt much better now that it was numb. He wondered how long that would last.

Mom and Brady returned a few minutes later. They handed out turkey sandwiches and bottles of water.

"It was really crowded in the cafeteria," said Brady. "There wasn't much food to pick from."

"This looks great," said Dad.

Sophie moaned and fluttered her eyes. Mom scooted a chair next to the hospital bed and pushed stray curls out of her daughter's face.

"Sophie. We're right here beside you. How are you feeling?" asked Mom.

Sophie's eyes fluttered again as she turned her head toward Mom. She squinted, trying to focus. "I feel foggy."

"That's normal," Mom said. "You just came out of surgery, so the anesthesia is still wearing off."

"Surgery?"

"Yes, honey. You broke your arm in the tornado. But you have a cast now and will be fine."

Sophie looked down at the pink cast on her arm and groaned. "Oh, yeah. Is everyone OK?"

Mom smiled at her. "Yes. Dad, Justin and Brady are all here. They're fine."

Sophie squinted at them. "Hi guys. What a storm, huh? Hey, what about Miss Doan and the rest of my class? Are any of them hurt?"

Mom cringed. "We'll find out more about them later. For now, just try to rest so that you can get better."

Sophie nodded and drifted back to sleep.

"The boys are probably exhausted too. Let's go home while Sophie is asleep," Mom whispered. "If we still have one!"

6

Missing

As the family returned to Moore, they drove beside the damage path of the tornado.

Dad slowed the car. "Where's our street?"

Justin looked out his window. The neighborhood where he grew up was barely recognizable. Street signs were gone. The trees that were left were stripped down to a few bare branches. The houses were just piles of wood and brick. Dad drove slowly down what he guessed was their street. He had to steer around a car door, a kitchen sink, and a shredded sofa. They could barely turn into their driveway because of the debris.

Justin felt sick. "Where's our house?"

They sat in the car just staring at the piles of rubble that had once been their home. Chunks of beige and blue dry wall were jammed against soggy pink clumps of insulation and wood. Three splintered stairs led up to nowhere. Only a few walls remained.

"Keep driving, Dad," said Brady. "This can't be our house."

Dad turned off the ignition and stepped out of the car. "No this is . . . *was* our house."

The rest of the family got out of the car very slowly. Justin felt his sense of security slip away as he walked in disbelief toward the rubble. Where would they sleep and eat and laugh and play? It was all gone. Was there anything left they could save? And then it hit him.

"Where's Tank?" he asked.

"Oh, no," Mom said, covering her mouth.

"We've got to find him," said Brady. "Tank!"

Dad looked at Mom and shook his head, but he began to holler too. "Tank!"

Justin walked over their crushed piano. "Tank! Here, boy! Come here, Tank!"

They searched and called until their throats ached. Dad saw one of their neighbors, Mr. Potters, sorting through the remains of his own house. He walked over and shook hands.

"You haven't seen Tank, have you?" Dad asked.

Justin looked up hopefully.

"No. Sorry. I'll keep an eye out for him, though." He looked over the destruction. "This is unbelievable, isn't it?"

Dad nodded. Justin kept listening, but returned to searching for his dog.

"Do you guys have a place to spend the night?"

"We actually haven't thought that part through yet. We've been so busy making sure our family was OK, that we're just now seeing the house."

"I heard about the kids' school." Mr. Potters said. "Mighty sad. How are your kids?"

"Sophie's in the hospital with a broken arm and concussion, but Brady and Justin just have minor cuts."

Mr. Potters nodded. "It could have been so much worse. The wife and I got to a friend's storm shelter just in time. We were packed in there like sardines, but at least we didn't get hurt."

"I'm glad. Looks like you wouldn't have been so lucky if you had stayed in your home," said Dad.

"That's the truth. I hear they are opening shelters all around to give people places to stay. Electricity is out in most of the town, but a number of churches are open and taking people in. By the way, where are you going to stay tonight?" asked Mr. Potters. "The wife and I haven't decided yet, but a gal walked by about an hour ago and said Trinity Church of the Nazarene has electricity and is setting up places to stay. We might go there."

"Maybe we'll head that way too," Dad said as he glanced at the setting sun. "I guess it will be getting dark soon. We probably should get going. It might be hard to drive with the street lamps out."

Mr. Potters nodded. "Suppose you're right. You folks hang in there."

"You too," Dad said.

Mom was carrying a few family photos in cracked frames back to the car. Brady was wiping mud off his old sock monkey. Justin was empty-handed. All he could think about was finding Tank.

"We'll sort through more stuff tomorrow," Dad said. "We need to get to a shelter before it gets any darker."

They piled back into the car.

Mom put her hand on the steering wheel. "Before we go, I think we should pray. There are probably a lot of hurting people right now. Some may have lost more than a house."

"Like their dog?" asked Brady.

"Pets . . . and maybe people," said Mom.

"As hard as this is, we have a lot to be thankful for," added Dad.

"What!" exclaimed Justin. "How are we supposed to feel grateful? Our house and our dog were both sucked up in the tornado. Our van probably went up in it, too. And everything we own. I prayed and the tornado still hit us. It doesn't seem like God was even listening."

"I understand," said Dad. "But if your mom hadn't gone to the school to get you kids, she would have been sucked up into the tornado, too. No one could have survived in our house. I'm sad about Tank, but the rest of us survived. That's a miracle."

Mom and Dad bowed their heads. Justin frowned until he noticed Brady watching him. He sighed and bowed his head too. Brady leaned on his brother's arm.

Mom cleared her throat. "Thank you, God, for keeping us safe, even in a tornado. We are grateful for Your protection. We pray that You will be especially close to those who lost someone in the storm. Please be with everyone in Moore in the days to come as we try to sort through all we've lost. Amen."

Dad started the car and pulled back onto the littered street. It was getting dark, so he had to rely on headlights to see. A few houses remained intact, but even they were dark and desolate.

"What is a shelter?" asked Brady.

Mom turned around in the car to face him. "I've never stayed in one before, but I think they have sleeping bags and blankets and pillows and a safe place to sleep. Pretend we're visiting friends or going camping."

"Can sock monkey go in with me?"

"Yes. I'm sure sock monkey is welcome."

"Will the shelter people be mad if we're dirty?"

"They will understand," Mom said.

"Are you mad that I'm dirty again?"

"No. I'm just glad you weren't hurt."

"Do you think Tank could fly in the tornado like a super hero?"

Dad's cell phone rang.

"Hello?" he answered. "Aunt Nora. Are you OK? Yes, we're fine, but our house isn't. We're headed to a shelter for the night. Really? Yes. Thank you. We'll be right over."

Dad stuck his phone back into his pocket. "Aunt Nora said the tornado passed right beside her house, but she's fine. Her house wasn't even touched. She said she didn't lose a single plate from her china cabinet."

"That's wonderful!" Mom exclaimed.

"She asked if we wanted to stay with her until we get things sorted out. I said yes. Any objections? It would be closer than Trinity Church."

"Sounds great, doesn't it, boys?"

Brady nodded. "I like Aunt Nora. She smells like mints."

"Yeah, sounds great," Justin said without much enthusiasm. He was happy Aunt Nora and her house were unharmed, but inside there was a part of him that was very angry at God. Why couldn't that be *their* house?

He prayed silently. "What about us, God? Why didn't You protect our house or school? Do You see us? Are You going to help?"

7
Action Hero

If only Justin knew how God was already on the move. News of the tornado began to spread and God began speaking to His children, asking them to be His hands and feet. People all over the United States began to hear God's call for *action*. People like Abby.

Abby collapsed onto the couch. Graduation ceremonies and the whirlwind of activities that followed made for an exhausting day. It was hard to believe she was done with high school. It had been an exciting, emotional day. It was time to unwind. She grabbed the remote and flipped through the channels.

A news reporter appeared on the screen. "At 3:00 today, an F5 tornado hit the city of Moore, Oklahoma. It was on the ground for nearly 40 minutes, leaving a 17-mile path of destruction."

Abby sat up straight. She recalled the seven years she lived in Oklahoma. Some of her friends still lived in Moore. Were they hurt? She planned on attending Southern Nazarene University in that area in the fall. Had the tornado reached the people there, too?

"Mom! Dad! Come quick!" she called.

The rest of her family poured into the living room and watched the television to see what had captured

Abby's attention. Images of destruction flooded the screen. They all dropped to the couch beside her.

"I want to go there to help," said Abby. "Right away."

"Hold on a minute," her mom said. "Let's think this through."

"But I'm done with school. What's holding me back? You always tell us to do what we can with what we have now."

"That's true."

"You say 'Don't wait for someone else to do it.'"

Her mom smiled. "You're right. I'm glad you listened."

"Then let me go help," Abby pleaded.

"I want you to help. But not by yourself." Her mom thought for a moment. "Maybe we could all go. And we could take supplies."

Abby jumped to her feet in excitement. "We could find out what they need and load up a bunch of it. I'll bet other people would drop off supplies, too."

"I'll start calling friends in Oklahoma to see what they need. I could even see if Nazarene Compassionate Ministries is responding. They might also know what we should collect," her mom said.

"We could post what we're doing on our Social Media sites and see if we get more donations that way. And I'll text my friends. *All* of us can call friends. And we can call the church, and . . ."

Her dad jumped in. "From the sound of it, we might need more than our SUV to deliver supplies. Tell you what. If you get lots of donations, I'll let you use one of the box trucks to get everything to Moore. Maybe this is one of the reasons we own a truck company."

Abby grinned. "Go ahead and get that truck ready. We'll fill it. I know we can."

The family began to tell everyone about their plan. They received a list of supplies that were needed and spread the word.

The next day, her dad parked a large, white box truck in their driveway and opened the back. Abby went to her dentist and mentioned what they were doing. She was surprised when he gave her a box filled with toothbrushes and toothpaste. She returned home and found that the donations were already pouring in.

Friends put bottled water, diapers, and plastic bins full of supplies into the truck. Friends of their friends delivered shampoo, soap, allergy medicine and disinfectant wipes. Even more people eagerly donated Advil and Tylenol, Band-Aids, Bibles, sunscreen and work gloves.

News reporters came to do a story about the relief effort. Abby watched her mom speak to the television reporters with ease. She was nervous when they asked her to speak on camera, but she sat at the edge of the truck and smiled.

"Moore seems like a really strong community and with the support of everyone else in the nation, they'll bounce back. I'm excited to be part of helping them to do just that," she said.

The video clip was on the evening news. Soon complete strangers were donating items. Her simple idea was growing. The compassion of the entire community was almost overwhelming.

Abby climbed into the truck and sorted through the growing mound of supplies. She prayed over the medicine, hoping it would ease physical pain. She walked past the huge stack of bottled water and found a box of blankets. They looked homemade. Abby fingered the fringe on a rainbow colored one. She imag-

ined the comfort the blankets would bring to people wet and chilled from the tornado. Her heart was full. It wasn't long before the truck was full too.

"Hey, Dad?" she said. "I think we're going to need another truck."

Abby and her family decided it was time to find a more convenient drop-off location so even more people could donate. After making some calls, they moved three box trucks to the parking lot in front of College Church of the Nazarene in Olathe, Kansas.

"Let's put signs on the sides of the trucks," suggested Abby. "Signs that let people know we love Oklahoma."

Her mom taped huge rectangles of red butcher paper on the sides of each truck. Abby grabbed a black marker and wrote "Olathe Loves Oklahoma" on each sign in large letters. She stood back to inspect her work.

"It's missing something," she said.

Her mom studied the signs for a moment. "Let's have people write a message and sign their names when they donate. That would make it even more personal and encouraging."

Two days later, all three of the box trucks were filled with supplies. Every sign was filled with signatures. Three families volunteered to help drive the supplies to Oklahoma. It was time to deliver.

8

Prayer Request

Justin didn't know about Abby's efforts. He slumped in a chair in the hospital waiting room while his parents filled out paperwork at the front desk. Brady bounced up and down on the teal padded seat beside him.

"Sophie gets to come home today! Sophie gets to come home!" he chanted over and over.

"We don't have a home, remember?" Justin muttered.

Brady's smile faded and he stopped bouncing. "I know." He picked at a Super Hero Band-Aid on his arm. "But at least she gets to leave the hospital. At least her head and arm are going to be OK. At least we still have our Sophie."

"Yeah, I'm glad about that too."

Brady pressed his forehead to his big brother's face and stared at him. "You don't look glad."

Justin pushed him back into his chair. "I'm very relieved about Sophie. I just can't seem to get happy knowing everything we own is gone."

"We each have a toothbrush and toothpaste," said Brady.

"That's because Trinity Church gave us crisis care kits."

"And they gave us each a shirt and shorts."

"Yeah."

"And they gave us work gloves and shovels."

"So we could dig through our smashed house," Justin grumbled.

"And they gave us plastic tubs and bags."

"In case we find anything of ours that we could save . . . which we haven't."

"But Mom said we would spend more time sorting through stuff once we have Sophie with us and don't have to keep driving to the hospital. Maybe we'll find some of our toys."

"I just want to find Tank. He's been gone two days. He really must have been sucked up into the tornado."

Brady started sniffling. Justin looked up and saw tears running down his pudgy cheeks. "Hey Brady, I'm sorry. I didn't mean to make you cry."

"I miss Tank too," Brady said rubbing at his eyes.

Dad strolled up beside them. "All right, guys. Let's go get your sister. The paperwork's finally done."

"Mom stroked Brady's hair. "Why are you crying? This is a happy day. Sophie gets to come home."

"But we don't have a home," said Brady.

Mom gave him a hug. "But we have our family. God will be our shelter. Hang in there, little man."

They walked through sterile, white hallways until they entered Sophie's room. She was sitting up on the bed, clean and dressed.

Brady's smile returned. He jumped onto the bed and squeezed her tight.

"Be careful of the cast," she said, but she grinned and hugged him back.

The rest of the family gave her hugs and gathered her plastic bag of medicine and belongings.

"Let's go get some lunch at Aunt Nora's house," said Dad.

"And then can I see what's left of our house?" asked Sophie.

"Are you sure you're up to that?" Mom questioned, stroking back her curls.

Sophie nodded. The family walked side by side down the hall.

"Wait! Justin!"

Justin turned and saw Lauren skidding toward him. He stopped.

"Can you do me a favor?" Lauren asked, panting.

"I suppose. What's up?"

Lauren caught her breath and looked at her feet. "My mom's not doing so well. She was in our house when the tornado struck, and most of it fell on top of her. The doctors . . . well, they still don't know if she'll make it." Lauren fought back tears. "I know you were praying when the tornado hit our school, and you talk about God and stuff. Could you . . . would you start praying for my mom? I don't know much about that sort of thing, but we . . . need God's help."

Justin nodded. "I'm sorry about your mom. I'll be sure to pray for her."

"Our whole family will pray for her," added Mom.

"Thanks," Lauren said. A tear trickled down her face. "Are you going to the school's end of the year reunion tonight?"

"I hadn't really thought about it yet," said Justin.

"I want to go, but it will depend on how Mom is doing. It's a good chance for us to say good-bye, since they had to cancel the rest of the school year. It will be strange though knowing that some of the kids won't be there. How sad that some of the third-graders died." She sighed. "I have to get back. Dad's not taking this well and he doesn't like to be alone. Remember to pray, please."

She whirled around and raced back down the hall. Justin's family huddled together and prayed for Lauren's mom in the hallway. Justin's confidence in prayers was still shaken, but he prayed anyhow. He squeezed his family tight, grateful that they were all alive and well.

Sophie was silent on the drive to Aunt Nora's house. She leaned her head against the window. Tears welled up in her eyes.

Justin studied her face. "Is this the first time you've seen all of the destruction? You were unconscious last time you drove through town, weren't you?"

Sophie nodded.

Brady patted her knee. "It looks like the Incredible Hulk went crazy here, huh?"

She nodded again and started crying. "This is all so sad." She tried to take a deep breath. "But what was your friend talking about? Were there really some kids in my grade that d-died?"

Mom turned around in her seat. "Oh, honey. I didn't want to tell you yet. Yes, there were some kids who didn't survive the tornado. I'm so sorry."

"How many? Who?" Sophie asked in a small voice.

"They haven't released all of the names yet. It sounds like there were seven kids, but I don't know for sure yet. It's heart-breaking, I know."

Sophie's sobs grew louder. "I can't go to the reunion tonight," she choked out. "I don't want to see who's missing. Not yet."

"We understand, Sophie," said Dad.

47

They pulled up into Great Aunt Nora's driveway. The older woman greeted them at the front door, hugging Sophie. She adjusted her bifocals. "I'm so glad to see you—pink cast and all." She turned to the rest of the family. "There are homemade cookies and peanut butter and jelly sandwiches."

"A peanut butter and jelly sandwich sure sounds good," said Mom. "Let's eat."

After lunch, they drove to the remains of their house. Sophie's jaw dropped.

"You told me it took a beating, but this . . . this can't be our house."

Mom hugged her. "If this is too much for one day, we can go back to Aunt Nora's place."

"Thanks, Mom. I just need a little more time."

Justin called for Tank and did a quick search before he returned to the car. He felt himself sinking in despair again. He pictured Lauren crying for her mom and Sophie crying for her classmates. "We need You, God. This is just too much for us to handle. Please show us You still care."

9
Lost and Found

The next day, Justin and his family returned to the remains of their house. They all pulled on work gloves. Dad gave each kid a plastic bag in case they found something in the rubble that they wanted to keep. Justin called and searched for Tank for almost an hour, and then began to dig for things to salvage. He found part of his dresser, tossed on its side. Two drawers still remained, partially filled with soggy clothes. He wrung out a pair of jeans and four T-shirts and jammed them into his black plastic bag.

"I found a toy," Brady exclaimed. He held the plastic action figure up high. "I knew his super suit of armor could survive a tornado."

Dad was yanking on the handle of something embedded in a branchless tree trunk. "I found my saw." He yanked harder. "But I don't think it will ever come out of this tree."

Justin walked over to his mom. She was sitting on a pile of bricks, flipping through the battered pages of a scrap book.

"This is the only scrapbook I could find," she said. "All of your baby pictures . . . all of Sophie and Brady's baby pictures . . . they're all gone."

"Maybe they just blew to someone else's house," Justin suggested.

Mom tried to smile at him, but failed. She squeezed his hand instead, placed the soggy scrapbook into a plastic tub and returned to her search.

Justin dug through more drywall and splintered wood. He imagined what the rest of the world was doing right now. He pictured them going about their normal lives, as if nothing had happened. Did anyone outside of Moore even know how his world had stopped?

Sophie dropped the door to their crushed microwave. "Who is Olathe?" she asked, pointing to the street.

Justin squinted. Three white box trucks were slowly moving down the street. Large red paper signs were plastered on each of them. They said "Olathe Loves Oklahoma" in handwritten letters.

"I drove through a town in Kansas called Olathe on one of my business trips," said Dad. "I wonder what that's all about." He nodded toward the three trucks.

The trucks puttered along until they were out of sight. The family continued sorting for several hours, until they were sore and dirty.

Mr. Potters waved at them. "Care to join me for some lunch? That Trinity Church of the Nazarene has a food station just down the street."

Dad wiped sweat off his forehead. "That sounds really good. Come on gang, lets' go eat."

They followed Mr. Potters on foot to a food station. People were standing in lines, picking up bottled water, sports drinks, sandwiches, chips and apples.

Justin took a sip of his Gatorade, and felt a tap on his shoulder. He spun around and smiled.

"Hey, Lauren," he said. "How's your mom?"

"She came out of her coma last night. The doctors think she has a good chance of recovering. You prayed for her, didn't you?"

Justin nodded.

"I thought so. I figured that was why she was improving. My Dad and I have been staying in the shelter at the Trinity Church of the Nazarene. They're the ones serving this food. Did you know that people from all over the United States have been sending money and supplies through Nazarene Compassionate Ministries to help us? Do you know how many Christians like you I've seen this week? They haven't been all preachy to us or anything, but I can tell they really care. They're different. Kind of like you."

"Huh?" Justin always had a hard time keeping up when Lauren talked.

"Not a bad different. You're just nicer than some of the other guys at school. You don't talk the same way they do—you know—like saying bad words or telling disgusting stories and jokes. Don't get me wrong, I'm not saying that I like you. I mean, I like you, I just don't like you like you. You know what I mean?"

"I think so?"

"I mean, you're a good friend, just not a *boyfriend*. I just like the way you act. And I'm guessing you act like that because of the God that you pray to. I'd like to know God. I want to know someone that makes you act like you do, and makes the people at Trinity Church of the Nazarene act the way they do. I want to know a God who is bigger and stronger than a tornado. I was thinking I'd ask the pastor or someone at the church how to become a Christian. Do you think that's a good idea?"

Justin grinned. He understood that part! "I think that's a great idea."

Lauren smiled back. "Thanks. See what I mean? You always know what to say. Maybe we can talk more about being a Christian later. I'm glad we'll be in Junior High together."

"Yeah. Me too."

Lauren turned and ran off. Justin kept smiling. She confused him, but he knew she was headed in the right direction.

Justin and his family finished eating and returned to their house. They sorted for three more hours, and still hadn't salvaged more than a few bags of belongings.

"The trucks with the red signs are back!" Brady shouted.

This time the trucks pulled off the main street and rumbled down a side road, eventually slowing to a stop. Three other cars pulled up behind them. The doors opened and 20 people of all ages began to step outside. Each of them wore work gloves, and they were smiling. A few of them started walking toward Justin and his family.

"Could you use any help?" asked a tall man.

Dad looked up. "Really? We're starting to wear down, so that would be great. If you find anything in one piece, let me know."

Four adults and several kids began to sort through the rubble.

"You're from Olathe?" asked Mom.

"Yes. A group from Olathe College Church of the Nazarene gathered supplies from people in our town, and drove it down to Trinity Church earlier today. We wanted to help wherever we could before we headed back."

"You gathered enough to fill three whole trucks?" Justin asked.

"There are a lot of people out there who want to help."

Brady stared at two of the girls. "You look the same."

One of the girls grinned. "That's because we're twins. I'm Miranda." She pointed to her sister. "That's Madison. What can we do to help?"

Brady squinted at her. "Do you know how to play hide and seek?"

"Sure."

"Could you play it with me? I've been working all day long and need a break."

"But we can't stop . . ." Sophie began.

"Actually, that's a great idea," Mom said. "You kids have been through enough to age anyone. Enjoy some time being kids, at least for a few minutes." She looked at the twins. "Do you mind?"

"Not at all," said Madison.

"Yes!" Brady exclaimed. "We have all sorts of hiding spots now!"

Brady, Sophie and Justin split up, hiding behind broken doors and soggy mattresses. The twins counted to 100 and began their search. They looked around for several minutes and finally found Sophie and Justin. They continued searching, but could not find Brady.

Finally, Miranda grabbed her sister's arm. "Wait a second. I hear him. Listen."

They heard faint thumping sounds near a pile of debris. Madison got down on her stomach and looked under a splintered door. Two dark eyes looked back at her.

"How did you get way down there so fast?" she asked.

Justin came up behind her. "Who are you talking to? I know where Brady's hiding, and this isn't it."

"But I see and hear someone under all these walls and wood," Madison said.

Justin got on his stomach and stuck his head through a gap. The thumping increased, and was accompanied by a faint whine. The eyes were barely visible under the rubble. Justin began to toss aside drywall, wood and debris. Sophie, Madison and Miranda joined in. Soon they uncovered a cracked bathroom sink and cupboard smashed sideways across a tub. The tub held several inches of dirty rain water. A filthy pug poked his head out of the cupboard and tried to bark. A pitiful whine came out instead.

"Tank!" Justin and Sophie yelled.

Tank whined again.

"Come here, boy," Justin called.

Tank squirmed, his tail thumping hard, but he couldn't budge.

"Look! His collar's caught on some metal from a pipe," said Sophie.

Justin carefully dug deeper until he could push the cupboard door open and twist Tank's collar free. He scooped up his shaking dog and carried him through the rubble. Their pug was much skinnier, but he was *alive*.

Mom, Dad and the Olathe crew gathered around the dog. Tank squirmed free, giving everyone slobbery doggy kisses and wagging his entire backside.

Justin pulled Tank into his arms and stroked his dirty head. "I know how you feel, Tank. It felt like God had deserted us. That He didn't really care. But He has been by us this whole time. He never forgot about us."

"Hey, people. Did you forget about me?" asked Brady. "I'm still hiding!"

Discussion Questions

1. What would you do if you heard a tornado siren and you were told that it was not a drill?

2. Would you ask God any questions after emerging from a tornado that destroyed your house or school? If so, what would the questions be?

3. Which character (person) in the story reacted to the tornado similar to how you would?

4. Name a time when it felt like God had forgotten you. Does He ever truly leave us? Why or why?

5. Do you think your faith in God would waver if you lost a family member or pet during a tornado? How might you allow God to strengthen your faith so that it remains intact even in a tragedy?

6. What were some of the ways that people helped the tornado victims in this story?

7. How old do you have to be to help someone in need?

8. What was the most surprising way someone helped out another person in this story?

9. What are some ways that you can help if a tornado or another type of disaster strikes again?

10. What was your favorite part of this story? What was your least favorite part?